# CHRISTIAN PREMARITAL COUNSELING

# Books by Paul J. Bucknell

*Allowing the Bible to speak to our lives today!*

+ Overcoming Anxiety: Finding Peace, Discovering God
+ Reaching Beyond Mediocrity: Being an Overcomer
+ The Life Core: Discovering the Heart of Great Training
+ The Godly Man: When God Touches a Man's Life
+ Redemption Through the Scriptures
+ Godly Beginnings for the Family
+ Principles and Practices of Biblical Parenting
+ Building a Great Marriage
+ Christian Premarital Counseling Manual for Counselors
+ Relational Discipleship: Cross Training
+ Running the Race: Overcoming Lusts
+ Genesis: The Book of Foundations
+ Book of Romans: The Living Commentary
+ Book of Romans: Bible Study Questions
+ Bible Study Questions for the Book of Ephesians
+ Walking with Jesus: Abiding in Christ
+ Inductive Bible Studies in Titus
+ 1 Peter Bible Study Questions: Living in a Fallen World.
+ Take Your Next Step into Ministry
+ Training Leaders for Ministry
+ Study Guide for Jonah: Understanding God's Heart

➡ Check out these valuable resources at
   www.foundationsforfreedom.net

# CHRISTIAN PREMARITAL COUNSELING

## Preparing the Two to Be One

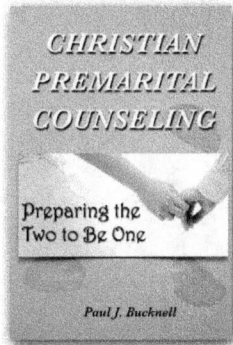

Rev. Paul J. Bucknell

Christian Premarital Counseling: Preparing the Two To Be One
by Paul J. Bucknell
Copyright 2011, 2014 by Paul J. Bucknell
All Rights reserved. Permission to make/modify/print forms and
handouts for your personal educational and counseling purposes.

Paperback
ISBN-10: 1619930293
ISBN-13: 978-1-61993-029-2

Also in digital format
ISBN: 978-1-61993-001-8

The NASB is used unless otherwise noted. The NEW AMERICAN
STANDARD BIBLE, (C) Copyright: The Lockman Foundation 1960,
1962, 1963, 1968, 1971, 1972, 1973, 1975, 1977, 1988


www.foundationsforfreedom.net
Pittsburgh, PA 15212 USA
For any questions, info@foundationsforfreedom.net

# Christian Premarital Counseling

# Introduction

## *Preparing the Two to Be One*

***Everything you need to conduct premarital counseling!***

I recommend Christian premarital counseling for every couple. Just think of it. The great God who designed male and female also designed marriage. He knows how marriage best works! Why not see what He has to say?

The question is, "How does one conduct premarital counseling?" Many have not received any training in this area. I faced this problem. As a pastor, I had to figure out how to conduct premarital counseling. The benefits of the counseling were plainly evident. Session by session, couple by couple, I finally figured out a plan. I have since then enhanced it and made these resources available to our readers. Everything one needs is included here.

This premarital counseling manual helps one understand how to handle Christian premarital counseling sessions step by step. There are not many premarital counseling materials around. This book aids pastors, elders and other church leaders involved in premarital counseling to challenge and prepare engaged couples to have good and godly marriages.

This series includes many handouts, worksheets and even a questionnaire for the couple to complete and pass back to the counselor. Suggestions for a few recommended books are provided, but those books are not closely tied to these resources, providing you the freedom to use your own suggested books. We aim at providing you the opportunity to edit and reshape the material for your own situation, but everything is already to use if you prefer. For example, you can put your church name on them, etc.

I do not know of any who marry with the hope of having a bad marriage. One can see by the festive manner in which the couple holds their wedding that they have much hope for their marriage. The question is, "How is the couple going to get there? Where are the good models for these young people? They are hard to find. The more the society and families deteriorate, the more a study of what God says about marriage is needed. Premarital counseling is best seen as a specialized discipleship course that enhances the truths relevant to establishing a good and godly marriage for the couple.

It is admitted that couples are often rather naive regarding their needs. Although the couple will not remember much, we as the counselors must help point out the obstacles that they might face early in their marriage and give them hope and means to overcome them. I find it rather amusing that in one of our premarital counseling appointments that the couple usually comes over right after a big argument. They do not want to come, but it is an appointment with the pastor. They still come. Guidance, love and hope sowed early into a couple's life brings much fruit.

The materials are designed with flexibility. They guide one through purposed conversations where the counselor is able to better know and understand the couple getting married. The first lessons are probably half occupied by getting to know the couple better. As the sessions progress, the couple is guided on how to converse with each other, resolve problems and appreciate each other. The counselor's responsibility is to help them face their early problems early on in a protected context so that they can by God's grace manage them well later on. Couples always will have difficulties to face and overcome. We show them how God can help them.

We meet six times before the wedding and once afterwards if they are in town. My wife, Linda, and I hold these meetings in our home. Our sessions are semi-private, that is, our children are apt to run by. Usually we do not require total privacy except on certain portions of the material. If we need more privacy, we arrange for it. By having the couple in our home, we are introducing them on how a godly family operates.

Since there is not much written out there on how to provide premarital counseling, I will share with you what I do for each session. My hope is that you take what you find and improve it! Feel free to copy and adapt the material for your own purposes. Each of these six sessions have a handout and, in many cases, forms to fill out. When the few charts from outside resources are used, we provide information on how to easily acquire them.

Rev. Paul J. Bucknell, Updated December 2011, 2014

# Pre-session Resources

For every course, there are many things to prepare. We have included several items here: a schedule, suggestions and a questionnaire. Remember many of these pages like a schedule and questionnaire can be downloaded in a better format. Don't be concerned with copying them from the book.

# Introduction of Premarital Classes and Forms

Premarital counseling for me has been a highlight of ministry. These sessions aim the couple in the right direction for a great marriage, but every session also brings benefits to our own marriage. This book is filled with practical advice from the beginning to the end. Although we have much advice to pass on, being married for more than 35 years, we retain a firm conviction that God's advice stands as most important. Each session's handout, therefore, is based on some key Bible teachings. In this section, we have included some general advice for the course as a whole.

This book consists of four parts: advice, session handouts, and activity forms along with occasional reading. Each session's resources are given in that order. The advice consists of many detailed instructions on how one can carry out the premarital counseling session. Feel free to make whatever adjustments your situation dictates. Session handouts are given out and discussed on the day used. The couple is expected to later insert them in the 3-ring folder provided by you.

Activity forms are given out in the session preceding their actual usage so that they can fill them out at home. Two examples: The questionnaire is distributed by the counselor, completed and returned before the first premarital session. The financial activity forms are distributed at the end of session #3 but discussed in sessions four and five. The completed activity forms should be collected before the session. Sometimes it is helpful for each spouse to see the other's form. This is doubly true for the the temperament profile and possibly the questionnaire.

My premise is that honesty is one key foundation to a good marriage. It is better to be open before the marriage so that there are no surprises later on. Revealing the truth can instill fear, but if the other spouse is hiding things from the other, then it is dishonest. Marriage is for life. One should know who one is marrying including any previous sexual encounters, health issues, abuse suffered, parental opposition and debt incurred. If one is willing to admit present frailties and past mistakes, then it allows one's to-be spouse to knowledgeably and fully committed to him/her.

All the session handouts and forms are available in pdf for printing. Handouts and activity forms are available in several formats for internet use or adaptation of the forms. You do not need to ask permission to edit, translate or otherwise adapt the handouts or forms. They are designed for your use and reprinting for counseling purposes (but not for sale). If there is inadequate time to discuss the form in the given session, one can finish discussing crucial content at the following sessions.

➡ **Suggestion**: For computer savvy couples, create a shared Dropbox where files can be placed, before and after completion.

The couple is asked to read the book: "*The Family: God's Weapon for Victory*" by Robert Andrews. This book provides a practical and yet biblical perspective of courting, marriage and family. You probably have your own book(s) that you want the couple to read. The suggested book is not linked to the counseling so it is easy to substitute.

One other resource that provides a fun way of discussing one's differences is the book, "*Your Temperament: Discover Its Potential*" by Tim LaHaye. There are many other personality forms, some quite extensive and expensive. Use whatever one that you are trained for and suitable. Beware, however, of using much time on this. Our goal for this activity is to understand how different God made each person, to appreciate the special benefits of a person's unique traits and to warn them of potential conflict. God's grace allows them to overcome these differences. Only remember your time is limited and some tests are not worth the high costs. Each of our suggested books can be acquired new or used. If you use LaHaye's chart, you can copy the charts from LaHaye's book for your teaching purposes. It is also involved directly on the internet. Encourage the couple to develop and use their own family Christian book library.

## ❖ Available downloads in appendix

Our downloadable resources really are a huge asset to this course. Active links for editing, copying and convenience are found via a link available in appendix 1.[1] The list of downloads is placed below to help you see how they fit into the teaching curriculum. These downloads have several benefits.

(1) All can be **modified**. Change the handouts or forms. Do you see a question you would want to add or modify on one of the forms? Change it! We give you the freedom to customize all these worksheets for your ministry so that you can most effectively teach and bless these couples. The doc format, for instance, allows you to add or delete the questions you want or add your church name!

(2) **Inexpensive and hassle free**. Feel free to make copies for students or clients. No need to report to us.

(3) **Convenient**. A copy of the forms are available in this book so that you can easily familiarize yourself with them, but they are also downloadable in a better format for printing, modified or not.

---

[1] Contact me (Paul) with any difficulty. Find the email address at the front with the book's information.

(4) **Modern.** Do you want to email someone the questionnaire? Then email the document you desire most convenient for them and you. We only ask that you refrain from posting them on the public web. Just email them please.[2]

## ❖ The list of downloads

The download list below is **according to when they are distributed**. Some, like the handouts, are used right in that session. But generally, the forms are distributed in the previous session so that they fill them out at home. They are supposed to get them back to you before the next session, providing you the opportunity to analyze the forms ahead of time.

One does not want to take time surveying the forms, such as the questionnaire, while they wait for you. This process does not always work, but it is great when it does! Using email makes it much easier to carry out. Effective use of time depends on a good strategy. If you hand them printed forms, then they can hand them back in that form or simply scan or fax it back to you. Do return the final forms back to them for their folders. This helps preserve opportunity for them to think about and further discuss these things on their own. Here are the handouts and forms.

---

[2] Placing them on your own Dropbox and providing a link is fine if not open to the public.

**Pre-Counseling Session**

Premarital Scheduling: pdf | xls/xlsx | docx
Premarital Questionnaire: pdf | doc

**#1 The Design of Marriage**

Handout #0: Establish Biblical Foundation: pdf | doc | epub

Handout #1: The Design of Marriage: pdf | doc

**#2 Principles of Godly Communication**

Handout #2: Principles of Godly Communication: pdf | doc
Form: Discovering One's Values: pdf | doc
Form: Discovering Your Expectations: pdf | doc

**#3 Wise Decision-making**

Handout #3: Wise Decision–making: pdf | doc

Reading: Advice for Engaged Couples: pdf | doc | epub

**#4 Finances & Marriage**

Handout #4: Financial Perspectives: pdf | doc
Form: Financial Perspectives: pdf | doc | epub
Form: Budget for First-Year: pdf
Form: Wedding Budget: pdf | doc

**#5 Understanding our Differences**

Handout #5: Understanding our Differences: pdf | doc

**#6 Preparations for Intimacy**

Handout #6: Exploring Sexual Intimacy: pdf | doc

---

**Download Hints**

➡ pdf: great for viewing and printing. Most computers can open them without any special software. One needs special Adobe Acrobat or alternative apps to edit.

➡ doc/docx: Editable with *Word* (Microsoft's app).

➡ pages: Editable with *Pages* (Apple's app).

➡ ePub: For reading or viewing. Need an ePub reader like iPad's iBook or Nook.

➡ xls/xlsx: Editable layout with Excel (Microsoft's app)

# Schedule of Premarital Classes and Forms

The following schedule, also available in a download in a spreadsheet (like Excel) or word processor for printing (Word), provides a general plan for what happens in a given session. The downloaded schedules have columns for checking off when distributed, collected, and other items like comments, etc. Details for each session is given later.

## ❖ Couple's names

- 
- 

## ❖ Before the first session

- Give and receive questionnaire before class #1
  - Form: Premarital Questionnaire: pdf | doc | pages
- Have them order on their own or provide it
  - The Family: God's Weapon for Victory by Robert Andrews
- Order now (them or you) #5
  - Your Temperament: Discover Its Potential by Tim LaHaye
- Order now to use later as gift or post-marriage
  - Building a Great Marriage by Paul J. Bucknell

## ❖ #1 The Design of Marriage

- Review HO#0 - introduce goals and expectations
  - Handout #0: Establish Biblical Foundation: pdf | doc | pages | epub
- Review HO#1 - Try to finish at least half.
  - Handout #1: The Design of Marriage: pdf | doc | pages

- Collect questionnaire; begin discussion

  - Get forms from them before your meeting so that you can first review.

## ❖ #2 Principles of Godly Communication

- Review HO#2 - Discuss

  - Handout #2: Principles of Godly Communication: pdf | doc | pages | epub

- Integrate questionnaire in your discussion (insights and warnings)

  - (From the questionnaire)

- Distribute Discovering Your Values

  - Form: Discovering Your Values: pdf | doc | pages

- Distribute Discovering Your Expectations

  - Form: Discovering Your Expectations: pdf | doc | pages

## ❖ #3 Wise Decision-making

- Review HO#3 - Wise Decision Making

  - Handout #3: Wise Decision Making: pdf | doc | pages | epub

- Review Values and Expectations forms

  - Get forms from them before your meeting so that you can first review.

- Distribute - Advice for Engaged Couples

  - Advice for Engaged Couples: pdf | epub

- Distribute Financial Perspective

  - Form: Financial Perspective: pdf | doc | pages

- Distribute Wedding Budget

  - Form: Wedding Budget: pdf | doc | pages

## ❖ #4 Finances & Marriage

- Review HO#4 - Financial Perspectives
  - Handout #4: Financial Perspectives: pdf | doc | pages | epub

- Review Financial Perspective
  - Get forms from them before your meeting so that you can first review.

- Review Wedding Budget
  - Get forms from them before your meeting so that you can first review.

- Distribute Budget for First-Year
  - Form: Budget for First-Year: pdf | doc | pages

## ❖ #5 Understanding our Differences

- Review HO#5 Understanding our Differences
  - Handout #5: Understanding our Differences: pdf | doc | pages | epub

- Review Budget for First-Year
  - Get forms from them before your meeting so that you can first review.

- Check plans on honeymoon
  - Assign to work out plan as needed

## ❖ #6 Preparations for Intimacy

- Review HO#6 - Exploring Sexual Intimacy
  - Handout #6: Exploring Sexual Intimacy: pdf | doc | pages | epub

- Check again honeymoon/budgets/harmony
  - Have a good honeymoon! (No handout! or gift of BGM)

- Confirm post-marriage appointment 7-10 months

# #7 Post- marriage

- Review their marriage; can they resolve

  - Handout #6: Exploring Sexual Intimacy: pdf | doc | pages | epub

- Distribute this book or others as desire

  - *Building a Great Marriage* (BGM) by Paul J. Bucknell

*See downloads for xls form*

# Premarital Questionnaire Form

To Be Kept Confidential
*See downloads*

**General Information**

Name _____

Other name _____

Address _____

City_____ State_____ Zip_____

Occupation _____

Cell phone _____ Other phone _____

Birth date _____

Favorite hobbies and sports_____

Educational background: _____
(List highest grade, degree or diploma)

How long have you been a Christian? _____

Do you have regular devotions?   Yes _____ No _____

What is your greatest struggle as a Christian?

_____

_____

# Premarital Questionnaire Form (2/7)

## Marriage Information

Fiancée's name _____

Married before? Yes _____ No _____

How long have you known each other? _____

How long have you steadily dated? _____

When were you engaged? _____

Do you have your parents' approval? Yes _____ No _____

Where and when will you be married? _____

By whom? _____

What city will you live in after you get married? _____

Will you then live by yourselves? Yes _____ No _____

Your future address and telephone if known:

How far have you gone on your wedding plans?

Haven't started____        Started____        Almost done _____

Have you made plans for your honeymoon?

Haven't started____        Started____        Almost done _____

Do you have any difficulties in planning for either your marriage, honeymoon or post-marriage days? Yes____ No____

   If so, please state in which area(s) you have difficulty.

_____

# Premarital Questionnaire Form (3/7)

## Background Info

Are you parents still living?      Yes _____   No _____   Only one _____

Where? _____

Occupation (or former if retired):

    Father _____      Mother _____

Are your parents Christians?  Yes __   No __?

If so, can you talk about your spiritual life with them?  Yes __   No __

Have your parents ever separated or divorced?   Yes _____      No _____

When was this? _____

Rate your parents' marriage:

    Unhappy _____   Average _____   Happy _____   Very Happy _____

As a child, did you feel closest to your:

    father (Yes ____), mother (Yes _____), or another (Who? _____)?

Rate your childhood :

    Very happy _____   Happy _____   Average _____   Unhappy _____

How many?      Older brothers _____   Younger brothers _____

                   Older sisters _____      Younger sisters _____

Who disciplined you?   Father _____   Mother _____

Were they strict?  Yes _____   No _____   Overstrict? _____

# Premarital Questionnaire Form (4/7)

## Health Information

Rate your physical health (check):

Very Good_____    Good_____    Average_____    Declining _____

Your approximate weight _____ lbs.    or _____ kgs.

Recent weight changes:    Lost _____    Gained _____

List all important present or past illnesses, injuries or handicaps:

_____

_____

_____

Date of last medical examination _____

Report results: _____

Have you recently had a medical examination especially with marriage in mind?  Results?

_____

Have you used drugs for other than medical purposes?  Yes _____    No _____

      If so, what kind? _____

Are you presently taking medication?  Yes _____    No _____

      If so, what kind? _____

Have you ever had a severe emotional upset?    Yes _____    No _____

      If so, when was the latest? _____

# Premarital Questionnaire Form (5/7)

Have you ever had any psychotherapy or counseling?  Yes _____  No _____

When and what for? _____

Do you have any fears or worries?  Yes _____  No _____

What are they? _____

Do you have any physical or emotional concerns?  Yes _____  No _____

If so, what are they? _____

Have you discussed family planning?  Some _____  None _____  Much _____

What are your conclusions? _____

_____

## Other Concerns

In what ways are your lifestyles, backgrounds and opinions similar?

_____

_____

_____

In what ways are your lifestyles, backgrounds and opinions different?

_____

_____

# Premarital Questionnaire Form (6/7)

Is there any pressure to get married, either by someone or some circumstance?

Yes _____  No _____

Why are you getting married?

_____

_____

Have you had any previous sexual experiences?   Yes \_\_\_\_  No \_\_\_\_

When? _____

If so, does your fiancé know of them?    Fully \_\_\_\_    Partially \_\_\_    Not at all \_\_\_

Have you ever suffered sexual abuse? If yes, how old? _____

Are there any other issues you wonder whether you should tell your fiancée?

Yes _____         No _____

Have you discussed standards on your physical relationship before marriage?

Yes _____         No _____

If so, what is this standard? _____

_____

What are your parents' ideas on this matter? _____

_____

In what areas do you find the greatest disagreements? _____

## Premarital Questionnaire Form (7/7)

Does your fiancée know you disagree on these things?

Yes _____    No _____    Somewhat _____

Do you see marriage creating any difficulties or stresses in your life?

Yes _____    No _____    If so, what? _____

Would you like to talk to me personally about some issue without your fiancée present?

Yes _____    No _____

What issue is that?

_____

_____

Date questionnaire completed _____

Signed

# Session #1 The Design of Marriage

**Christian Premarital Counseling**
Preparing the Two to Be One

The first session starts with dinner! Usually each session has 1 ½ to 2 hours of time. This first session is extended. We obviously totally disagree with the concept that we should separate our ministry from our lives. We talk over dinner, hopefully make the couple more comfortable, informally train them on the family and hope they also take up hospitality in their homes (1 Peter 4:9).

Each session starts with prayer. These six appointments are arranged early on. The schedule is not only for them but also for my own planning. We can change appointments, but it is much easier to plan them in before the wedding draws near. Meeting every 2-3 weeks seems ideal, but they can be more closely scheduled if necessary. Sometimes a spouse might need to fly in to make an appointment. The sessions should be held every four weeks for continuity. They should not be spaced too closely together to gain maximum benefit. Exceptions can be made for some situations, especially when they live far apart from me or each other.

*Time Distribution:*

• **Invite them over your house for supper (1 hour).**
Casually eat together at home with all the children, learning more about each other. They catch a glimpse how my wife cooks for a large family, how to talk at the table and how the children take turns cleaning up.

- **Go over the Premarital Questionnaires with them (10-30 minutes).**

I often interweave this time into our informal conversation before dinner (unfortunately this means Linda, my wife, will not be there). Acknowledge their time used in completing it. Usually I look for facts to help me understand them and potential trouble points. These points help direct future conversations. For example, if they have a broken family background, I need to spend much more time sharing what a biblical family is like. If they have committed fornication or easily get angry, then these things should be dealt with, as the Lord leads.

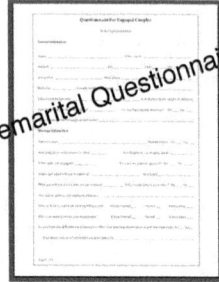

One group desired further information for the couple to provide. You might consider these items.

- Credit report
- Blood work (required in our state)
- DMV report (driving record)
- Criminal report

These reports could come in very handy. We cannot assume everyone is honest. Besides, we just might forget to ask certain questions. If a counselee's blood is HIV positive, what ramifications does being positive or other significant problems create for the couple? These become significant issues.

- **Handout a folder (5')**

Give each of them a folder (with 3-prongs) with pockets. As time allows, make a label with their names on it and the course name. Print the handouts in different colors as you please.

Please note, in the first session two teaching handouts will be passed out: *Establishing a Biblical Foundation for a Loving Marriage* (overview) and *The Design of Marriage.* Usually each session will have one teaching handout (1 two-sided page) along with homework assignments and returned assignments. The questionnaire is kept private and not returned. Refer to it as needed throughout the counseling sessions. They are very helpful to detect possible problem areas.

- **Distribute and discuss Introduction & Handout #1, The Design of Marriage**

  **(1) Overview (5')**

    (Note the diagram in the introduction that serves as an index).

    - First introduce the course with handout #1 and introduce the six sessions. I mention that I am willing to help provide resources for any area of need and that I am willing to meet with them individually as needed.
    - #1 The Design of Marriage
    - #2 Principles of Godly Communication
    - #3 Wise Decision-making
    - #4 Finances & Marriage
    - #5 Understanding our Differences
    - #6 Preparations for Intimacy

  **(2) Glory of marriage (15') (Part of Introduction)**

  Marriage is wonderful! I want them to know it and aim for having a great marriage. I show them how a great marriage is tied to having and living by a Biblical perspective of marriage. As we start off, we need to walk by faith. Through this introduction I show them the importance of premarital counseling that helps the couple get a Biblical perspective. This also makes them reassess the importance of church and their personal spiritual growth for the future.

### (3) Gaining a Biblical Perspective (50') Handout #1

Because of dinner and having them join our family devotions (this time only), I rarely finish the second page on *The Design of Marriage*. It is partly deliberate. We were busy getting to know each other. I want to emphasize this section a bit more in the next session.

### (4) Quotes on a Biblical Marriage (5') Handout #1

- Quickly read the quotes and make appropriate comments.

- **End with prayer requests and prayer**

Have the husband-to-be pray first, then his fiancé, my wife and then I close. I only ask them to pray for their marriage. This too is training. Usually I ask them to pray for certain matters brought out from our conversation together. For example, "Ask God to give you a beautiful marriage."

- **Assign homework**
  (1) Assign *"The Family: God's Weapon for Victory"* by Robert Andrews to read over the course of counseling sessions. Personal and refreshing, *The Family* helps a couple in the courting and premarital stages. Feel free to choose your own book, only make sure you prepare this ahead of time.
  (2) Give them the two forms to fill out:
      * Discovering_Values: pdf | pages
      * Roles_Husband-Wife: pdf | doc | pages
  (3) Challenge them to meet together in God's Word and prayer during the week. I will check on them next time. I want them to get in a habit of this. If they individually do not meet with the Lord, then they will need much more help here. For now, it might be sufficient to have them discuss the reading and pray together.

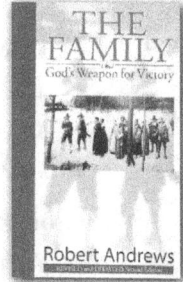

Note #1

Several formats such as pdf, doc, pages refer to documents you can download from the purchase of this book. Pdf is great for printing but not for changes. All are set up in 8 1/2 by 11. Doc is an editable page for Word. Pages is an editable page for Apple's Pages program (app). We encourage editing for more effectiveness.

Note #2

Although I highly recommend my book, *Building a Great Marriage*, most of the book would best be studied after the couple is married. The first part, Faith, can serve as an excellent complement to this premarital counseling book as it clearly shows the biblical foundation for marriage. We, however, recommend it as a post-counseling or wedding gift. Three main sections: Faith, Forgiveness and Friendship provide the foundation, recovery principles and the means to gain a deep enriching marriage. Study questions included!

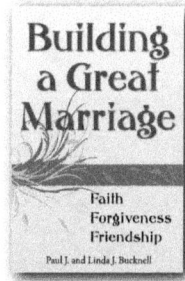

# Establishing a Biblical Foundation for a Loving Marriage

**Christian Premarital Counseling**
Preparing the Two to Be One

## ❖ An Overview

Any good marriage will have a solid foundation. The Lord exhorts us to conduct our marriages after His teaching because He is the chief inventor and designer of marriage. Our goal is to build a biblical foundation for our marriages that our lives would reflect God's goodness and order and so provide help to our families and others that have lost hope.

*"Unless the LORD builds the house, They labor in vain who build it."*
(Psalms 127:1)

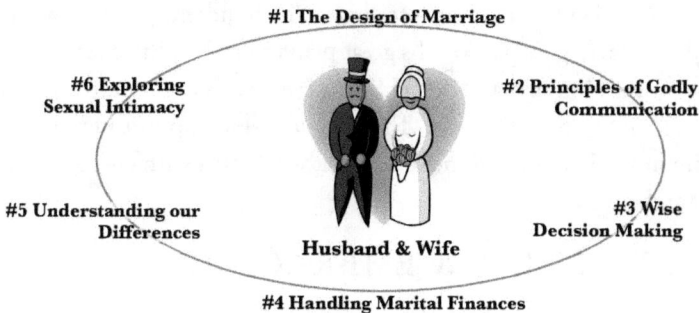

**#1 The Design of Marriage**

**#6 Exploring Sexual Intimacy**

**#2 Principles of Godly Communication**

**#5 Understanding our Differences**

**#3 Wise Decision Making**

**Husband & Wife**

**#4 Handling Marital Finances**

## ❖ The Glory of Marriage

Most the people getting married are absolutely convinced that they are going to have the greatest marriages existing. The facts are that the majority of people are enduring terrible marriages or are getting divorced. What in your marriage is going to make you different?

The romanticists believe good marriages just happen. The godly person knows it happens by much discipline and hard work. God has a plan but we need to strive to reach it. The more we understand God's design for marriage and affirm this purpose for ourselves, the stronger our marriages will be.

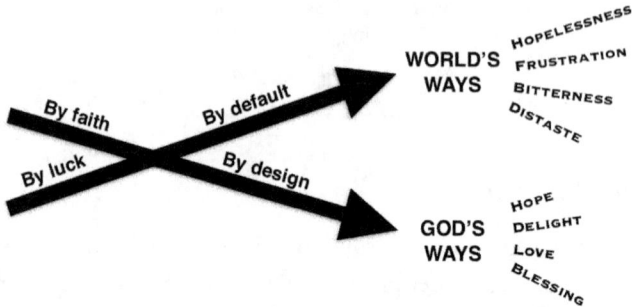

God graciously wants to share His abundant goodness with you. Marriage is part of His great plan to do that. But He wants you to set Him first and obey Him as He reveals different truths for your lives from His Word. This is your lifelong opportunity to know Him more. Below are some topics that we discuss with engaged couples to share these truths.

God graciously wants to share His abundant goodness with you. Marriage is part of His great plan to do that. But He wants you to set Him first and obey Him as He reveals different truths for your lives from His Word. This is your lifelong opportunity to know Him more. Below are some topics that we discuss with engaged couples to share these truths.

**PSALM 91**

## ❖ REJECTING & EMBRACING

### • Two steps

(1) Acknowledging and rejecting worldly ideas about marriage, relationships, sex and life.

*"How blessed is the man who does not walk in the counsel of the wicked, Nor stand in the path of sinners, Nor sit in the seat of scoffers!" (Psalms 1:1)*

(2) Understanding and affirming biblical ideas about marriage, relationships, sex and life.

*"But his delight is in the law of the LORD, And in His law he meditates day and night" (Psalms 1:2).*

# The Design of Marriage

**Christian Premarital Counseling**
Preparing the Two to Be One

## ❖ Gaining a Biblical Perspective

Before asking why a couple wants to get married, we need to ask what are God's purposes for marriage. Even more foundational, we need to think through the reason God created man and woman.

## The Couple

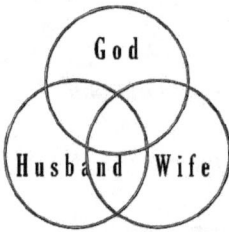

Most people recreate their marriages after their own purposes in life. They think of what they want and then pursue it. If we seek pleasure and happiness, we will miss God's goal for our marriage.

• What is God's purpose for your marriage?

• How does marriage and family relate to each other?

## The Husbands

Men rarely think about what God wants for their lives. They tend to innately follow their wants and pursue their desires.

• What is God's purposes for man?

• Is this the same in the New Testament era? Is there any change?

• How do you know (Colossians 1:9-13; Mat 28:18-20; Titus 2:2, 6-8)?

The husbands need to proactively seek God's grace and purpose for their marriages and families if they are to establish good marriages.

# The Wives

Woman was created before the entrance of sin into the world.

- How did the creation of woman fit into God's overall purpose for mankind?
- Is this the same in the New Testament era? Is there any change?
- How do you know (Gen 1:18-25; 1 Tim 2:1-15; Tit 2:3-5)?

The wive's major calling from God are to be helpmates to their husbands. They need to adjust their time, life and schedule so that they can help their husbands excel.

## ❖ Quotes on Marriage

- *Marriage is God's invention.*

- *Marriage is an excellent gift, a most beautiful reward.*

- *Marriage is to be the most intimate and satisfying of relationships.*

- *Marriage is designed to supply comfort in a cold and wicked world.*

- *Marriage is fashioned to be the context of morally and spiritually replenishing our lives.*

# Discovering Your Values

| Man | | What is true of you? Answer appropriate side. Circle A to Agree and D for Disagree. | Wife |
|---|---|---|---|
| A   D | 1 | I tend to argue my point when someone disagrees with me. | A   D |
| A   D | 2 | If someone asks me to do something that I don't like, I try to figure a way around it. | A   D |
| A   D | 3 | I tend to shout when I get upset. | A   D |
| A   D | 4 | I agree with the Bible teaching that the wife is to submit to her husband. | A   D |
| A   D | 5 | The husband is the leader in the home even if he does a lousy job. | A   D |
| A   D | 6 | It is important to spend less and save money. | A   D |
| A   D | 7 | It is easy for me to accept criticism. | A   D |
| A   D | 8 | I hardly ever get real mad. | A   D |
| A   D | 9 | I like to spend time talking to others. | A   D |
| A   D | 10 | I sometimes lie or deceive. | A   D |

| A  D | 11 | I believe the Bible's viewpoint is the final say. | A  D |
|------|----|--------------------------------------------------|------|
| A  D | 12 | A couple must agree on everything. | A  D |
| A  D | 13 | It is okay if my spouse doesn't improve his/her character. | A  D |
| A  D | 14 | I like things neat and organized. | A  D |
| A  D | 15 | Each spouse should have his/her own free time each week. | A  D |

Please note: These statements are not to be presumed right or wrong.

# Husband and Wife Marital Roles

| Man | | What do you expect in a marriage?<br><br>Answer appropriate side. Circle **A** to Agree and **D** for Disagree. | Wife |
|---|---|---|---|
| A    D | 1 | Both husband and wife should work outside the home and contribute. | A    D |
| A    D | 2 | The mother should be at home with the children. | A    D |
| A    D | 3 | Preschool is a good option so the wife can work. | A    D |
| A    D | 4 | Each spouse should be able to manage his/her own money. | A    D |
| A    D | 5 | A spouse can watch a program even if the spouse disagrees. | A    D |
| A    D | 6 | The wife should do all of the housework and cleaning. | A    D |
| A    D | 7 | The couple should regularly go to church and pray together. | A    D |
| A    D | 8 | The husband should politely protect the wife from in-law interference. | A    D |

| A D | 9 | The wife should nag the husband to get him to fix something. | A D |
|---|---|---|---|
| A D | 10 | The husband is responsible to make house repairs and care for yard. | A D |
| A D | 11 | The husband should keep the accounts and pay bills. | A D |
| A D | 12 | The husband should always initiate sexual intimacies. | A D |
| A D | 13 | The husband has the last word in everything. | A D |
| A D | 14 | The husband is responsible to lead spiritual matters. | A D |
| A D | 15 | The wife should normally care for all the meals. | A D |

Please note: These statements are not to be presumed right or wrong.

# Session #2: Principles of Godly Communication

**Christian Premarital Counseling**
Preparing the Two to Be One

The time structure of the second session will be repeated in the following sessions. After some short conversation, we will sit down and open in a word of prayer. This prayer is not a trivial matter. We are looking for God to bring breakthrough in their lives. Each time the truth of God is presented we are wholly dependent upon the Holy Spirit for these changes. We are also seeking wisdom for ourselves to know what to and not to say. These sessions are very limited. We need God to prepare the couple and work in them.

After this I begin with questions on how they are doing as a couple. Some couples might be shy and not be open about their disagreements. Probe a bit deeper into their answers until you get to know the couple and can know their situation. This lesson is largely focused on basic communication skills. One has to see whether the husband talks and, if so, how much and about what. Make sure that the couple talks in the right way, without criticism and arguing. Some counselors openly say that arguing is good. It is not. Yes, arguments get the issues out in the open, but it does not do it in a proper way. Besides, there are other deeper issues that are hidden behind the now anger-covered scenes.

## ❖ Time Distribution:

1. Get further acquainted; Check on past assignments (10')
   Check on their buying the book and starting to read (hopefully

together). See if the husband led a Bible study or prayer time with his fiancée.

2. Finish lesson #1: The Design of Marriage (5-30')
Don't skip this section. Finish it next session if need be. In any case, briefly review it. You will need to keep coming back to it.

3. Discuss any Homework (5-10')

   (1) The two questionnaires should have been returned to you now (if not earlier). You can discuss them during the lesson or now. The two sides are given so that you can take the two pages (guy and gal) and match the answers. Where you see a big difference, these could point to potential conflicts. Discuss. If time is limited, see if they can work it out before next class.

   (2) Ask them if they got the book and started reading it?

   (3) Did they read God's Word and pray together?

4. Discuss Handout #2 (60')

   (1) Motivated by Love (Ephesians 5:22-33)

   (2) Follow up lesson #1 by showing how the husband and wife need to rightly communicate with each other. Expose any critical talk.

   (3) The Touch of Grace and Truth (John 1:14)
   One always needs to treat the other as if they never sinned and better! This is true for our conversation. It is not false. We choose to speak as God has instructed us. However, we must remember that does not mean we cover up our problems. Some people have not learned how to talk lovingly about problems. They need to learn how (don't focus on the results of the conversation but on trying to identify the problem and solution together before the Lord).

   (4) Guided by Biblical Principles (Ephesians 5:1-21)
   Assign them to pick out different phrases in the passage that would help shape their conversations. They are to get their standards from the scriptures. They need to spend time in God's

Word together to gain those values. (Take example from their Bible study last week).

5. End with prayer requests and prayer (10').
6. Assign homework (includes specific applications of what you taught them as well as filling out forms, sometimes together and sometimes alone).

➡ Keep reading, *"The Family: God's Weapon for Victory"* by Robert Andrews.

➡ Distribute the reading for the next session or later discussion.

- Advice for Engaged Couples (4 pages; 2 pages questions)
  - Physical relationships
  - Parental relationships
  - Special opportunities
  - Living wisely

# Principles of Godly Communication

**Christian Premarital Counseling**
Preparing the Two to Be One

## ❖ Motivated by love (Eph 5:22-33)

*"Wives be subject to your own husbands, as to the Lord. For the husband is the head of the wife, as Christ also is the head of the church, He Himself being the Savior of the body." (Ephesians 5:22-23)*

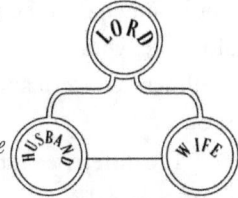

Your goal is to build up each other. This becomes one of your chief life goals no matter what else happens. This is expressed in the framework of our callings as husband or wife.

### • Husband

Constant love provides a secure relationship allowing for further growth in the wife.

### •Wife

Faithful respect and support for the husband enables God to work more wonderfully in and through his life.

*People communicate not only through their words or the lack of words but also through their actions and facial expressions.*

## ❖ The touch of grace and truth {John 1:14}

*"But speaking the truth in love, we are to grow up in all aspects into Him, who is the head, even Christ" (Eph 4:15).*

**Grace is treating people and especially our spouse better than he or she deserves.**

**Truth demands that we consistently understand and maintain standards from God.**

*"And the Word became flesh, and dwelt among us, and we beheld His glory, glory as of the only begotten full of grace and truth" (John 1:14).*

## ❖ Guided by biblical principles (Eph 5:1-21)

Our communication with our spouses should not be much different from another brother or sister. Let your words be filled with politeness, godliness, concern and desire to build up your spouse.

*Some of your best conversations will occur while you discuss God's Word and pray together.*

The difference is that our opportunity to express ourselves increases due to frequent daily exchanges allowing for more in depth conversations.

- Pick out at least five guidelines for healthy conversations from Ephesians 5:1-21.
- Discuss your standards in light of God's standards.
- What do you do if you have offended the other or been offended?

*Effective daily devotional time along with meditation of the holy scriptures are essential to a godly and beautiful marriage.*

# Advice for Engaged Couples

Engagement is one of the most exciting stages for a couple. Each moment is heightened by great expectations of what it will mean to begin their new life on their own. Many couples are engaged for from six to eighteen months. Special attention will help protect and assure the most from this time. Let's focus on four issues during this wonderful time.

## ❖ (1) Physical relationship

The Hebrew wedding during Jesus' time kept the couple apart until the bridegroom would arrive in a surprise visit and take her away to his home. Many cultures today have radically different ways of doing the engagement. Most engaged couples want to spend as much time as possible together. That mutual attraction for each other is normal, but a man and woman must guard their physical relationship.

There are various standards of what is permissible and what is off limits. It is important, however, to set definite guidelines that conform to the scriptures and everyone is comfortable with. Anything that even mildly goes against the conscience of either one must be avoided.

The scriptures set clear guidelines against fornication (sexual intimacy before marriage). Engagement is not marriage. Completely refrain from sexual intimacies. This is critical to the foundation of the marriage. (Otherwise, how can one know that he/she really loves you and not just your body?)

Sexual purity is not difficult for most Christian couples to accept. What people disagree on is how this relates to other physical contact. A couple should agree to standards of conduct. Perhaps share with their parents but at least with another couple for keeping accountable. The reason for this advice is to create standards that keep everyone honest. One's standards should not be anything we try to hide from others (this usually means something is not quite right).

Standards can start off right in the evening but slide downward very quickly. These standards should reflect that petting (touching in intimate places), heavy kissing and rubbing are all pathways to sexual intimacy and should be avoided. Agreed upon standards will help keep each one vigilant to refrain from such contact. If you enjoy entertainment, what you watch and hear should also be pure and consistent with your standards.

Here are some suggested guidelines:

➡ Do not spend long times alone with no one else around (in his place or hers).

➡ Do not lay down together, even if fully clothed.

➡ Hold hands, quick kisses, short hugs, nothing that will stir the physical desire of the other.

➡ Continue to carry on friendships with your own friends.

➡ Pray together regularly.

Here are some important points. Be open and honest with each other. Make and keep the commitment to maintain and expose any violation of those standards. Share the standards with someone you trust.

If one person senses that the other is not keeping to the standard, then he or she is obligated to speak up. The other needs to properly respond with apology and correction.

All standards should express one's deepest holy desires. For example, if the woman felt uncomfortable with that kind of hug, then it should be discussed and added to the 'wait' list.

Most importantly, the standards are to be positively thought of. God wants you to use this time to focus on developing your relationship. Don't allow your culture to regulate your standards. You must do that. The more physical touch is allowed, the more the relationship becomes focused on sensual pleasures begging to be fulfilled. By holding off, one is able to freely develop a solid personal relationship focused on knowing one another.

• • • • ● ● ● ● • • • •

☐ Have you openly talked about standards during this time of engagement? Could you both share what you were comfortable with? Was the other one listening?

☐ Have you agreed to certain standards and to keep each other accountable? If so, write them down.

## ❖ (2) Parental relationships

Keep great relationships with your parents. They are happy for you and want to be involved in helping you make a good start. Older children are getting engaged and so parental expectations might differ greatly from younger children.

The younger the couple, the more directive the parents expectations will be: be at home by a certain time, clear communication as to where one is, etc. Since the engaged person is still a son or daughter, he or she should try to understand the parents' expectations and fulfill them.

If there is disagreement, don't get upset. First, remember it is only temporary. Second, think of it as God trying to pass some special advice on to you before you are on your own.

Try to understand not only what your parents are saying but why they are saying it. Ask them, "Why is it that you think that is so important?" Ask them in order to understand their values and not to pressure them to change their mind. This is one meaning of honoring your parents (Ephesians 6:1-3).

$$\bullet \; \cdot \; \cdot \; \cdot \; \bullet \; \bullet \; \bullet \; \cdot \; \cdot \; \cdot \; \bullet$$

☐ List any potential problems you might have with your parents/in-laws.

☐ Any action plan to deal with them?

## ❖ (3) Special opportunity

The engagement is a special time to start off right. By that I mean the way you relate to each other now, join church activities, handle your time, or deal with pressures will pretty much shape what happens in your marriage.

When I was engaged and met with my special girl, we often had Bible study and prayer times. We used a good portion of our together time to make sure we formed values that matched the scriptures. When engaged, a person's heart is much more easily molded. The habits of prayer and valuing what God values will be taken right into your marriage.

No couple will always agree, but they can have similar values. This is the time to see what you do value and make sure both your values match the scriptures. This will greatly protect and bless your marriage. The more you work through these areas before you are married, the less arguments you will have.

For example, if your fiancee thinks it is important to be at every church meeting and you do not, then talk about it now. Ask, "Why is it important for you to be at every meeting?" Get to know each other on this value level. Otherwise, during this time you might tolerate going to each meeting because you are with him, but this will become a future problem. This is true with all sorts of issues.

Do not fear tensions. Learn what different values you both have. Examine the scriptures and see what one should value. Or perhaps, how the same values might work out a bit differently due to different perspectives.

• • • • ●●●● • • • •

☐ Engagement is a special time! Do you have any special plans deepening your relationship with God or with each other? If so, how?

☐ Are there any areas that your fiancé does things that you aren't too exited about? Have you asked about why he/she likes those things?

## ❖ (4) Live wisely

The engaged couple can experience wonderful times together. What one does and does not do can shape the marriage including: spending habits such as eating out a lot, watching a lot of movies, etc.

If during the engagement, the couple carries on expensive dating, then they will expect to carry on this pattern in their

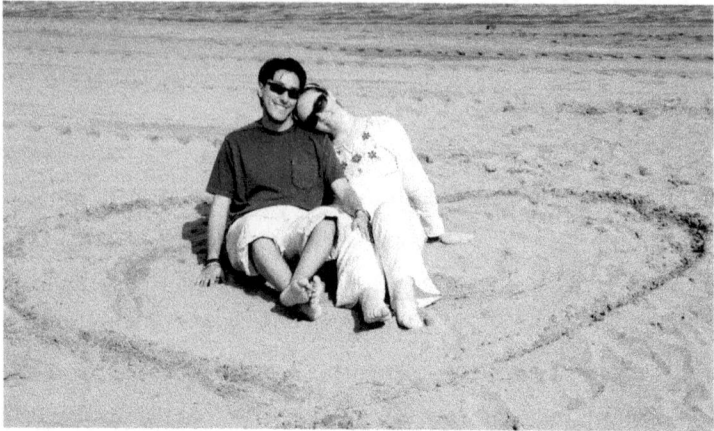

marriage. It is better to step into a lifestyle that both are comfortable with during the engagement so that after marriage, there are no unrealistic expectations to deal with. If you give to missions, make sure you tell the other.

Let's look at one more example. What if you are in the habit of watching a movie every night at your parents' house (not good to be alone in your own place - check above standards). That might be fine now because you value being with each other. But how do you envision your life after marriage? The same?

Or should you now work through whether you will volunteer one night doing some special activity that God put on your heart? Anticipate your future along with what God wants for your lives. Share those anticipations with your partner so he or she can envision what this might mean.

• • • • ●●● • • • •

☐ Have you openly talked about standards during this time of engagement? Could you both share what you were comfortable with? Was the other one listening?

☐ Have you agreed to certain standards and to keep each other accountable? If so, write them down.

# Session #3: Wise Decision Making

**Christian Premarital Counseling**
Preparing the Two to Be One

The couple must positively use the scriptures to guide their decisions and conversation. They will differ, but each opinion is to be respected. One needs to go to God's word to better understand why one should make a certain decision.

## Time Distribution:

- **Discuss any Homework (5-20').**

➡ Any forms from last week? (Discuss now or during lesson.)

➡ Are they reading the book? Anything interesting?

➡ Read God's Word and pray together?

- **Discuss Handout #3 (60')**

(1) **Plan ahead**
Don't get caught off guard. Look ahead and see when stressful times will arise or hard decisions coming up. Pray and discuss ahead of time. Remember they are just getting to know each other.

(2) **Handling misunderstandings**
There are two kinds of problems measured by their intensity: Common and serious. Discuss how the couple should and will handle disagreements. What to do when one offends the other? What to do when you offend another?

(3) **Read aloud and comment.**
Read aloud, "Words express...." from handout at an appropriate time.

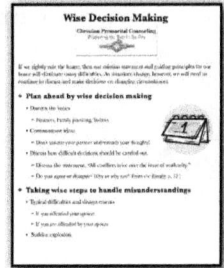

**(4) Discuss Family Planning (see page 2 of handout)**

This is one pertinent issue that is not to be left to the wedding night to decide! The scriptures are clear on how God wants to bless marriages through having children. Historically, the couple should understand that the church did not accept the notion of family planning, that is, they considered it immoral. Leave the last section as homework. For more reading.

http://www.foundationsforfreedom.net/Topics/Family/
Parenting030_Birth_Control.html

- **End with prayer requests and prayer (10').**

- **Assign homework**

  (1) Discuss family planning at home and observe your ability to discuss this important issue.

  (2) Keep reading, "*The Family: God's Weapon for Victory*" by Robert Andrews.

  (3) Fill in the forms below for the next session. Return them before the session.
    - Financial Perspectives: pdf | doc | pages
    - Wedding budget: pdf | doc | page
    - First year budget: pdf | doc | page

# Wise Decision Making

**Christian Premarital Counseling**
Preparing the Two to Be One

If we rightly rule the home, then our mission statement and guiding principles for our home will eliminate many difficulties. As situations change, however, we will need to continue to discuss and make decisions on changing circumstances.

## ❖ Plan ahead by wise decision making

- **Discern the issues**

  ➡ Finances, Family planning, In-laws

- **Communicate ideas**

  ➡ Don't assume your partner understands your thoughts!

- **Discuss how difficult decisions should be carried out.**

  ➡ Discuss the statement, "All conflicts arise over the issue of authority."

  ➡ Do you agree or disagree? Why or why not? (From the Family, p. 72.)

## ❖ Taking wise steps to handle misunderstandings

- **Typical difficulties and disagreements**

  ➡ If you offended your spouse

➡ If you are offended by your spouse

- **Sudden explosion**

---

### Words express our inner being

- Wrong words wound as in a battle. People frequently use words to manipulate others.

- Right words expressed at the right times are beautiful. They express true thoughts, feelings and sentiments. They are only possible when love motivates that person's heart and when he or she lives open before the Lord.

- We disguise sin not only from the Lord but also from ourselves and our spouse. Sin produces a veil over our relationship which places a barrier between each other provoking many misunderstandings.

- People who live after God's own heart are humble and forgiving rather than blaming and accusing. They find themselves building up others rather than trying to justifying themselves or meet their own needs.

---

## ❖ Family planning

- What do people typically think about having children?

- What does the Bible say about having children?

*"Your wife shall be like a fruitful vine, within your house, Your children like olive plants around your table. Behold, for thus shall the man be blessed who fears the LORD"* (Psalm 128:3-4).
*"Behold, children are a gift of the LORD; The fruit of the womb is a reward. Like arrows in the hand of a warrior, So*

*are the children of one's youth. How blessed is the man whose quiver is full of them" (Psalms 127:5).*

- Should we want to regulate the arrival of children?

- Is birth control moral? What attitude toward children and God might we display when we choose birth control?

❖ **Do you agree before the Lord?**

- Your views towards having children

- Your views toward birth control

# Financial Perspectives

| Man | | What is important to you? Answer appropriate side: 'V' for Very important, 'I' important, 'Unimportant' and 'D' for Disagree. | Wife |
|---|---|---|---|
| V I U D | 1 | Purchases over $50 should be discussed between the spouses. | V I U D |
| V I U D | 2 | One should never go into debt. | V I U D |
| V I U D | 3 | Purchase a used car to save money. | V I U D |
| V I U D | 4 | Live on a budget. | V I U D |
| V I U D | 5 | Regularly tithe (ten percent of income to the Lord). | V I U D |
| V I U D | 6 | Save for a house so at least 30% can be put down. | V I U D |
| V I U D | 7 | Life insurance. | V I U D |
| V I U D | 8 | Saving for vacation. | V I U D |
| V I U D | 9 | Spouses should have joint bank accounts. | V I U D |
| V I U D | 10 | Each spouse needs his own free money. | V I U D |

| | | | |
|---|---|---|---|
| **V I U D** | 11 | Keep the thermostat set cooler to save money. | **V I U D** |
| **V I U D** | 12 | Medical insurance. | **V I U D** |
| **V I U D** | 13 | Having the newest computer or gadget. | **V I U D** |
| **V I U D** | 14 | It is okay to leave a balance on the credit card. | **V I U D** |
| **V I U D** | 15 | Giving extra to missions, poor, etc. | **V I U D** |
| | | List anything else very important to you not mentioned above. | |
| | | | |
| | | | |
| | | | |

Please note: These statements are not to be presumed right or wrong.

# Wedding Budget

Do your best to estimate income and expenses for the wedding. If a budget is done elsewhere, that is fine. Just make sure it is done early on and adjust one's expectations.

## ❖ Wedding savings

Our purpose is to help you see what is available for your wedding.

- **Husband**  _____

    (include dedicated wedding savings, contributions from work, etc.)

- **Wife**  _____

    (include dedicated wedding savings, contributions from work, etc.)

- **Family**  _____

    (include all cash or in form of payments from both sides of the family)

- **Other**  _____


- **Total wedding income above** _____ **(total)**

# ❖ Wedding expenses

Our purpose is to gather all significant wedding and honeymoon expenses. Don't count twice.

- **Facilities** _____

    (include wedding, reception hall, tent, etc. )

- **Gowns**  _____

    (include all ones you pay for , men and women, etc.)

- **Ceremony** _____

    (include pastor, invitations, candles, etc. )

- **Food**  _____

    (include meal, snacks, drinks, reception,etc. )

- **Rings**  _____

    (include rings and other jewelry, etc. )

- **Photos**  _____

    (include all photo taking, video, etc. )

- **Flowers**  _____

    (include flowers and decorations, favors, etc. )

- **Rings**  _____

    (include rings and other jewelry, etc. )

- **Travel**  _____

    (include traveling expenses you pay for, rentals, etc. )

- **Miscellaneous** _____

    (include everything not included above )

- **Honeymoon** _____

    (include all honeymoon costs)

- **Other**  _____

    (whatever not above )

- **Total Expenses** _____ **(add all expenses )**

    Make your personal conclusions here.

## • Summary

It is always better to have a less expensive wedding than go into debt for the wedding and pay the costs later. If parents insist on more guests or certain provisions, then they should be expected to help cover the costs.

**Total Wedding Income** _____

**Total Wedding Expenses** _____

**Balance** _____

# First Year Budget

Do your best to estimate income and expenses for the first year (12 months). Adapt as needed.

## Income

Husband's job(s) _____

Wife's job(s)        _____

Gifts                     _____

Other                   _____

- **Total income above**   _____
- **Total savings available** _____

---

## Expenses

Our purpose is to gather your major first year expenses. Do not count things twice.)

- **Housing**        _____

    (rent, mortgage, real estate taxes)

- **House utilities**       _____

    (house gas, electric, water, sewer, oil, etc.)

- **Personal utilities** _____

    (phones, cable, wifi, laundry, etc. )

- **Transportation**       _____

    (auto, bus, plane, taxi, parking, gas, repairs, etc. )

- **Food & supplies**_____
    (food, things, etc. )

- **Lifestyle**          _____
    (clothes, eating out, travel, etc. )

- **Insurances**      _____
    (auto, medical, life, etc. )

- **Taxes**          _____
    (IRS, state, city, any significant, etc. )

- **Loan payments**          _____
    (Payments on Student, personal, other loans (not housing) )

- **Tuition & fees**_____
    (school, club, not counted above )

- **Charity & gifts**_____
    (family, church, other, etc. )

- **Other**          _____
    (moving, uniform, furniture, car, bike, )

- **Total Expenses**_____ (add all expenses )

| | |
|---|---|
| Total Income _____ | Savings _____ |
| Total Expenses _____ | Debts _____ |
| Balance _____ | |

- **Make your personal observations here.**

_____

# Session #4: Handling Marital Finances

**Christian Premarital Counseling**
Preparing the Two to Be One

Couples often argue over how to handle their finances. It was okay when they made their own decisions! The husband can still do that (and the wife should understand and appreciate that), but he is not wise to do it without his wife's input. The reason to make them one is to gain extra wisdom.

Get into the touchy areas. See if they are both committed to tithing, how they use credit cards, debt in general, etc.. Remember this session builds on the former ones that discuss good communication and decision making. Finances is another area for them to discuss!

These premarital sessions are times where I discuss sensitive topics so that might so that the couple is not later surprised. I would rather they go into marriage knowing these things rather than resenting them later.

This is a good time to discuss budgets (see forms), honeymoon planning and wedding budget. It is good to see if they have thought about their first year's expenses.

Couples should not go into debt for the wedding. That would only put more pressure on the marriage (of course, it is not proper either). Couples are to be content with what they have and live within their means. Buying more than they have is a sign of covetousness and idolatry (Ephesians 5:5).

Forms are given outside of the session to save time and give them time to discuss it together if they want. They are to fill out forms separately and then compare.

## *Time Distribution:*

- **Discuss any Homework (5-10').**

    ➡ Reading the book? Anything interesting?

- **Pass out and discuss Handout #4 (60') - Handling Marital Finances**

    ➡ **Financial guidelines**
    Talk through these discussion points.
    Suggest they read Ron Blue, Larry Burkett or David Ramsey's books.

    ➡ **Financial questions**
    Go through the form: *Financial Perspectives*.

    ➡ **Go over wedding budget.**
    Review their *Wedding Budget* form their own form or their own. Use it to make appropriate comment. If they are within the budget, then I move on.
    Rule: if you do not have money, then don't spend! Suggest alternatives - simpler wedding.

    ➡ **Go over first year's marriage budget.**
    Review the *First Year's Budget* form. Discuss any concerns. Help them see any possible problems and difficulties.

- **End with prayer requests and prayer (10')**
- **Assign homework**

➡ Discuss any particular financial issue that needs further discussion.

➡ Keep reading, *"The Family: God's Weapon for Victory"* by Robert Andrews.

➡ Distribute the personality form or test that you prefer. We suggest something lighter such as a copy of charts pp. 93-94 from Tim Lahaye's *"Your Temperament: Discover Its Potential?"* You should have secured your own copy and copied the charts. One circle chart is for one's self evaluation and two others: one is for the fiancée and another for a friend.

Great to familiarize yourself with the book or have them purchase their own. Some pastors like big expensive tests. Feel free to use them. I prefer the simpler which fosters discussion in the saved time. He offers his own tests– (timlahaye.com) though much more expensive.

# Handling Marital Finances

**Christian Premarital Counseling**
Preparing the Two to Be One

Some believe that money is the magic of a happy marriage. They are totally wrong. This is the teaching of materialism which believes that the satisfaction of one's own needs is the chief goal of life. This idolatrous teaching encourages a person to put his or her trust in something other than the One True God.

## ❖ A Few Financial Guidelines

- In 1985, the level of household debt relative to disposable income reached a postwar high of 88% to over 100% in later years.

- Debt sentences you to a lower standard of living in the future.

- The Bible does not say God is obligated to bail us out of debt.

> *Believe it or not, differences in financial matters is the prime reason for marital problems.*

- Lenders push as much of the risk to the borrower as possible.
  - You can spend money any way you want, but you can only spend it once.
  - Have you ever learned to trust the Lord for a financial need?
  - What do you think of insurance?

- What ideas do you have about savings?
- One guaranteed good investment is to pay back all high cost debt.
- Giving 10% of our income to the Lord's work is a basic level of giving rather than a high one.
- Merely putting a credit card in a potential user's hand will lead the person to spend 34% more.

"**Don't worry, Honey. I can handle it.**"

## ❖ A Few Financial Questions

- Do you need a budget?

➡ How flexible are you with it?

➡ What purpose does it serve?

- Who will keep order of the finances?

➡ Any problems with that system?

- How do you look at debt and monthly payments for products?

# Session #5: Understanding Our Differences

**Christian Premarital Counseling**
Preparing the Two to Be One

We have discussed decision making and ways to resolving conflict, but it is helpful to realize why one's spouse might have differing opinions. After all, if the couple is going to have a successful marriage, then they need to learn to appreciate and positively look at their fiancée. By understanding differences between male/female, personalities, gifts and varying backgrounds, then one can better appreciate why their mate is so different from them.

Some counselors prefer to use more expensive and sophisticated tests. I have found that so much time and money can be used that the whole point of the session can be missed. Emphasize the way one gains appreciation of each other by each person's individual unique contribution. They need to be aware that they cannot do without each other. (That was the reason to record Adam's naming of the animals).

The fiancé's commitment to their mate will work together with the realization how his/her to-be spouse so wonderfully meets his/her needs and helps spurt him/her forward into better knowing each other. Some feel more comfortable with a more sophisticated testing device. If so, use it! Just keep focused on the lesson.

Tim LaHaye has provided some of these forms in his books on temperament. These charts came from *Your Temperament: Discover Its Potential.* You should receive the temperament forms back before the session so that you can tally them up. Tallying does not take long, but it is necessary to get a general sense of what each of them are like and to see the opposites.

By seeing how different the two are also helps point out potential problems. Positively looked at, if one appreciates one another, then one will take advantage of the other person's gift! Encourage them to buy and read the book.

How do I tally the sheets? I tally up the points in each quadrant. I ignore the 1,2,3's. Each 4 gets one point and each 5 gets two points. This helps show the strength or weakness of each area and how much stronger or weaker it is than the other. I focus on the two stronger quadrants but also try to spot how weaknesses might make the couple prone to some problems.

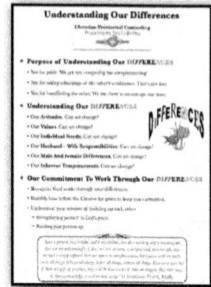

## *Time Distribution:*

- **Discuss any Homework (0-10')**

  ➡ Any followup on the financial questions?

  ➡ Are they still praying and reading God's Word together?

- **Pass out and discuss Handout #5 (75') - Understanding Our Differences**

  ➡ **Purpose of Understanding Differences**
  Several reasons: warn them of potential problems and appreciate the unique gifts in the other.

  ➡ **Understanding Our Differences**
  Differences can bother us if we do not rightly appreciate our mate. We will, after all, spend our lives with our partner.

  ➡ **Go over the charts**
  Spend time going over your observations of the charts and answering any questions. Integrate your observations in the previous two points.

  ➡ **Our Needed Commitment**
  The commitment needed to bind the couple together is the most important aspect of marriage. Both need to love no matter what. Conclude by reading 1 Corinthians 13:4-8a together.

- **End with prayer requests and prayer (10')**

- **Assign homework**

  ➡ Finish *"The Family: God's Weapon for Victory"* by Robert Andrews.

➡ Have them positively pray for each other through the week. Pray so that they build up each other by identifying weaknesses and strengths and seek God's blessings on them.

# Understanding Our Differences

**Christian Premarital Counseling**
Preparing the Two to Be One

## ❖ Purpose of Understanding Our DIFFERENCES

- Not for pride. We are not competing but complementing!

- Not for taking advantage of the other's weaknesses. That's not love.

- Not for humiliating the other. We are there to encourage our mate.

## ❖ Understanding Our DIFFERENCES

- Our **Attitudes.** Can we change?

- Our **Values.** Can we change?

- Our **Individual Needs.** Can we change?

- Our **Husband – Wife Responsibilities.** Can we change?

- Our **Male And Female Differences.** Can we change?

- Our **Inherent Temperaments.** Can we change?

❖ **Our Commitment To Work Through Our DIFFERENCES**

- Recognize God works through your differences.

- Humbly bow before the Creator for grace to keep you committed.

- Understand your mission of building up each other.

➡ Strengthening yourself in God's grace.

➡ Building your partner up.

> *"Love is patient, love is kind, and is not jealous; love does not brag and is not arrogant, does not act unbecomingly; it does not seek its own, is not provoked, does not take into account a wrong suffered, does not rejoice in unrighteousness, but rejoices with the truth; bears all things, believes all things, hopes all things, endures all things. never fails but if there are gifts of prophecy, they will be done away; if there are tongues, they will cease; if there is knowledge, it will be done away."*
> *(1 Corinthians 13:4-8, NASB).*

# Session #6: Exploring Sexual Intimacy

**Christian Premarital Counseling**
Preparing the Two to Be One

This last session aims to blend all the main session points together. By now, the counselor has seen the strengths and weaknesses of the couple. Encourage the couple to rightly face those problems so that they might have a strong marriage.

Our culture conveys so many wrong things about sex. Churches at times do too. In this session we largely want to paint a beautiful picture of what is good and lovely in its proper context. By reviewing the main questionnaire, we should be able to see if there are any significant problems. If there were, they should have been brought up earlier.

For example, the couple might have shared some physical intimacies with each other or others in the past. Someone might have STD (sexually transmitted disease such as venereal diseases and HIV). These issues must be dealt with before the marriage. Because marriage is built on intimacy, there is no way one can have a strong marriage and keep such significant matters hidden from one's spouse.

If these problems are stated before marriage, the partner still has an option to know what the person is really like, then there will not be any resentment. (Look carefully at the Premarital Questionnaire for any red flags.) Both the man and woman are to present themselves to each other as a virgin. If there have been girl or

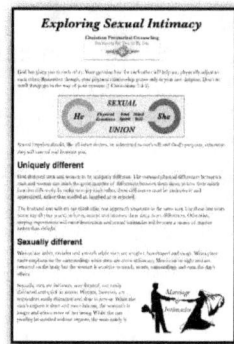

boyfriends but abstinence from sex and heavy petting, I do not force this issue to be brought up.

This session is a followup on the differences mentioned in the previous session. Differences show up in how the man and woman's sexual needs, responses and expressions. Emphasize the need for men to go slow (be romantic).

Usually, the wedding is not far off at this point and try to make this last session a bit shorter and less involved (unless it has to be). I share with them that we are there 24/7 now and in the future as needed.

### Time Distribution:

- **Discuss any Homework (5-10')**

⇒ Should have finished reading the book. Overall response? (There are questions in the book that can be used if desired).

⇒ Make sure their honeymoon is planned.

⇒ Discuss wedding plans.

⇒ Discuss and plan a one year follow-up session.

- **Pass out and Discuss 3 page Handout #6 (50') – Exploring Sexual Intimacy**

⇒ Explain the beauty of marriage and sex as an expression of that oneness. God designed it to work together in a blend of mystery and beauty.

⇒ Warn of emphasis on sex in our culture. Do not use pornography or sensual movies to stimulate. Sex is much more than getting together. We need to cultivate great relationships.

➡ Highlight the differences of the couple in the area of romance. This expands the former section on differences between men and women. It might be hard to speak about some of these items. We need to say what needs to be said.

➡ When the couple has been raised in big families, these differences will not cause so much problem. But if the guy doesn't have sisters, then there can be major problems. Speak about menstruation, and how the guy needs to patiently wait during these times.

➡ Pick out a few areas of conflict from the provided examples that you guess might become problems for this couple. Add your own from your own experience.

➡ As time allows, go over page #3 of the handout, "*Raising Children God's Way.*"

• **End with prayer requests and prayer (10')**

• **Assign homework**

➡ Plan any further meetings as needed. Mention that you will have one more meeting in about 10 months time. Put it in your appointment book now!

➡ See if there are any special wedding or honeymoon concerns.

➡ Give any other assignments that might be helpful such as "Raising Children" if there was insufficient time. We have two great books that can help.

➡

\* Godly Beginnings for the Family
*Godly Beginnings for the Family* helps parents start right: filled with lots of practical advice for pre-birth, birth and post-birth

accompanied with reading, handouts and clear illustrations on early training. Most things Paul and Linda have learned through careful training of our eight children.

* Principles and Practices of Biblical Parenting
The idea is simple. God is the Designer. Parent His way. We are not experts or perfect parents. We are humbled by our past failures. Our confidence is that by applying God's principles to family life He will restore any family to its glorious design. Principles and Practices of Biblical Parenting explains not only what God says about raising a godly family, but why those principles from God's Word work. With eight children Paul and Linda have had much hands-on practice!

# Exploring Sexual Intimacy

**Christian Premarital Counseling**
Preparing the Two to Be One

God has given you to each other. Your genuine love for each other will help you physically adjust to each other. Remember though, your physical relationship grows only as your love deepens. Don't let small things get in the way of your oneness (1 Corinthians 7:3-5).

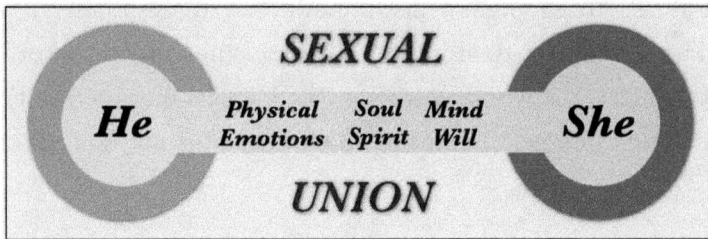

*SEXUAL*

*He* — Physical Soul Mind / Emotions Spirit Will — *She*

*UNION*

Sexual impulses should, like all other desires, be submitted to one's will and God's purposes, otherwise they will control and frustrate you.

## ❖ Uniquely different

God designed men and women to be uniquely different. The outward physical differences between a man and woman can mask the great number of differences between them down to how their minds function differently. In order to enjoy each other, these differences must be understood and appreciated, rather than scoffed at, laughed at or rejected.

The husband and wife do not think alike nor approach situations in the same way. Use these first years (some say all your years!) to learn, accept and treasure these deep down differences.

Otherwise, varying expectations will cause frustration and sexual intimacies will become a source of tension rather than delight.

## ❖ Sexually different

Women are softer, rounder and smooth while men are rougher, box-shaped and tough. Wives place more emphasis on the surroundings while men are more utilitarian. Men focus on sight and are centered on the body, but the woman is sensitive to touch, words, surroundings and even the day's affairs.

Sexually, men are initiators, very focused, not easily distracted and quick to arouse. Women, however, are responders, easily distracted and slow to arouse. While the man's orgasm is short and more intense, the woman's is longer and affects more of her being. While she can possibly be satisfied without orgasm, the man rarely is.

*Marriage & Intimacies*

## ❖ Common problems and solutions:

- The husband tends to focus on the outward beauty of his wife and his desires so that he forgets to care for the various needs of his wife.

   Solution: Go slower. Be patient. Learn to take time and enjoy delighting in your woman.

- When a wife becomes cold and unresponsive, Satan brings temptation to look elsewhere.

   Solution: Men must remember: looking at other women with desire is adultery (Matthew 5:28). Look at this time as one where God is coaching you to show your love by patient understanding of your wife, even if she is in the wrong.

- The wife can use sex to control her husband or teach him a thing or two.

   Solution: Work to bless the other. Revenge is not ours but love (1 Thessalonians 5:13). Never use sex as a tool to manipulate the other. When upset, do your best to work through the issues. Pray.

- Men and women can both become inattentive to the partner's sexual and emotional needs.

   Solution: Desires for sex can fluctuate due to many things. Worries, relationship problems, babies, hormones, busyness can all interfere. Make time to discuss, pray and be together. Men tend to neglect this talk part that helps resolve problems and builds emotional unity.

## ❖ Raising Children

**The church has drifted along with the society away from its biblical moorings. Only God's Word provides the hope, strength, love and wisdom to raise godly children.**

- While sex is enjoyable, this feeling is not the main focus of the sexual relationship. Sex is for expressing and developing intimacy. From this intimacy children come into the world (cf. Psalm 133; John 15:8). God has designed the family as a pleasurable way to continue His work.

- Children are great! They are not a bother, but God's great blessing. They usher the couple down into a responsible relationship where they are trained to love and care for others. As the forms of self–centeredness are set aside, they can speed on their way towards maturity.

- Abortion is a tragic expression of selfishness. It will always be illegal in God's world. Using fetal tissue resulting from an abortion is profiteering from murder victims. This is modern cannibalism.

- The parents, not the Sunday School teacher, nor Christian schooling nor the pastors, are overall responsible to train their children in godliness. This training must include both daily example and instruction (Deuteronomy 6).

- Parents must correct their children. This requires consistency, gentleness, firmness as well as clear instructions and punishments. They make sure the children feel uncomfortable expressing their evil nature and comfortable with a life of self-control. Hebrews 12 boldly says that if parents do not discipline their children, then they simply don't love them.

- The state of pregnancy is not a disease even though birth

often takes place in a hospital room! This grand process can hardly be rivaled in its intricate design and beauty. Breast feeding is superior to and easier than giving a baby a bottle. A working mother is often too stressed out or tired to provide the attention a little one needs. No agency can replace the mother's presence.

- Don't spoil your children. It is virtually impossible for them to develop deep gratitude to God, parents or others when they receive more than they can appreciate. Remember politeness differs from gratitude.

- God is in charge of caring for your needs. Don't let money get in the way of your worship of God. Worrying is a sign that you doubt God's care for you. He doesn't guarantee that His care will meet up with your expectations, but it will be sufficient to complete His good will.

- We should think of the family as a mini–church. The father is overall responsible for declaring God's truth and leading the others in worship and obedience. He serves as a pastor to the family and can look to grace for that wisdom and fortitude. The family forms a body where everyone has a part. Chores are an expression of their service in that community.

# Appendix 1: Chapter Downloads

The downloads are available below in one or more formats for your convenience. Instead of have many long links for the printed page, we provide a link to the downloadable page with active links. Bookmark this: bit.ly/1qERuEN If you have any questions, please contact Paul at the email address on page 4.

**Pre-Counseling Session**
> Premarital Scheduling: pdf | xls/xlsx | docx
> Premarital Questionnaire: pdf | doc

**#1 The Design of Marriage**
> Handout #0: Establish Biblical Foundation: pdf | doc | epub
> Handout #1: The Design of Marriage: pdf | doc | epub

**#2 Principles of Godly Communication**
> Handout #2: Principles of Communication: pdf | doc | epub
> Form: Discovering Your Values: pdf | doc
> Form: Discovering Your Expectations: pdf | doc

**#3 Wise Decision-making**
> Handout #3: Wise Decision Making: pdf | doc | epub
> Reading: Advice for Engaged Couples: pdf | doc | epub

**#4 Finances & Marriage**
> Handout #4: Financial Perspectives: pdf | doc | epub
> Form: Financial Perspective: pdf | doc
> Form: Budget for First-Year: pdf
> Form: Wedding Budget: pdf | doc

**#5 Understanding our Differences**
> Handout #5: Understanding our Differences: pdf | doc | epub

**#6 Preparations for Intimacy**

Handout #6: Exploring Sexual Intimacy:  pdf | doc | epub

# Appendix 2: Making Wise Decisions Before Marriage

Paul J. Bucknell

How does one build a marriage based on God's will? Here is one person who asked!

> *"Hello, my name's Heidi. I am engaged to an awesome man named Peter and we want to have a marriage based on God's will for our lives and have him as #1 in our lives. We realize you are incredibly busy, so we won't take up much of your time, but do you have any information we could have or know of any on line stuff we could find? I would be grateful for any thing you could do. God bless you and your work. Bless you, In Jesus Name."*

Let's look at five areas a person needs to focus on to live out God's will for his or her marriage. We are concerned with building the right marital foundation for a beautiful family that pleases God. God's way is always the best way! Let's search through these areas of our lives to examine what needs to be done. An outline of the five points precedes the extended discussions.

### 1• Decision: Discerning God's spouse for you

We first need to settle on who God wants us to marry. The details can get a bit complicated, but it sure is worth thinking through. You will, after all, be married all your living days! This decision settles who you will need to love or listen to.

### 2• Preparation: Readying your heart

After deciding who one would marry, one then needs to get ready for marriage. This does not so much concern your wedding ceremony but your hearts. God has hopes that you will use this time to work out those major problems in your lives so that you will not bring pain and frustration into your marriage.

### 3• The Plan: Becoming a Christ-centered home

Of course, we need to build our marriage as the Architect of marriage has designed. We need to spend regular time with Him to see what steps we need to take next. We need to build into our lives the necessary disciplines to implement His plans.

### 4• Team work: One Heart and Mind

Marriage is team work. The husband and wife are not only to enjoy getting married but also being married! Many know this but get frustrated by wrong perspectives on how marriage should work out. We will show you how.

### 5• The Vision: Making plans for the future

We also need to plan ahead. We can be so busy with present matters that we give little thought of the ideal or projected home that we want to build. Present pressures and desires lure us into the wrong pathway. Keeping the final picture before us greatly helps us make the necessary decisions now to reach those plans.

---

## Expansion of Discussion Points

Let's now look at each of these areas in more detail.

# 1• Decision: Discerning God's spouse for you

Most couples tend to jump over this first step. We get so excited about someone loving us so, that we couldn't believe God's will is anything but him or her! He is 'Awesome'! Even still, though, we must be open whether this is God's person for you. Go through the following steps. You will not regret it.

First, are you both Christians? If not, then you should not date, court or consider marriage. Your question assumes you are, but one never knows. Our emotions at times block out God's perspective.

Second, do both of your parents agree to your courtship and marriage? Again, many couples go astray when they are not willing to submit their marriage to their parents' decision even if they are non-Christians. God can and does work through non-Christian parents. We must not despise God or our parents because of this fact.

> *"Children, obey your parents in the Lord, for this is right.*
> *HONOR YOUR FATHER AND MOTHER (which is the*
> *first commandment with a promise)" (Ephesians 6:1-2).*

Third, check and see if you are both physically, emotionally, spiritually, etc. ready for marriage. Our parents sometimes consciously and always subconsciously think about these things, but it is good for the couple to see what areas need to be worked on before they get married too. If we look at these things objectively, then we can muster up that extra discipline to get where we need to be at. Often our parents do not know some special aspects about our lives.

We need to be completely honest with our parents and potential partner. We should divulge our financial affairs (incurred debt), social obligations (is there that other girl left hanging out there, sexual affairs, divorces), physical problems (STDs, cancer, etc.), and other issues that might influence the evaluating of what God's will is. For example, one partner might be HIV positive. How is this going to affect their lives? Blood tests for getting married? Having children? We want nothing hidden that is later revealed.

Fourth, are you spiritually compatible? If the woman is much ahead of the man spiritually, then there are going to be much frustrations for that marriage. It would be better for the man to take a year alone with the Lord without the pressure of an engagement and grow. He could take special time serving the Lord in the local church and have special times of Bible memory, meditation and prayer. In order to be a good husband, he needs to be a spiritual leader before they get married. This does not mean he is a deacon, but it does mean he loves the Lord and knows how to disciple others.

Lastly, one needs to see whether God is leading them in the same direction. We need to understand that the woman chiefly gets her guidance from her husband. Once she is married, her goal becomes to make him a great man, successful in all that God has called him to be. But if before marriage, she senses God has a special mission or purpose for her life, she must contemplate what that is. At times, it will be fulfilled in her future life with her husband. It is difficult for her to struggle through these questions alone in her heart. She should talk about them with some trusted people.

Many of the above issues have to do with the timing of marriage; some have to do with whether one should get married at all. Those who really seek God's will, will offer up their potential marriage to God as a sacrifice. They will choose to do what God wills for them because they believe it is best.

We should mention that if any of these areas are neglected or ignored, one is already building a very poor base for their marriage. This is the foundation of a house. If they marry not in the Lord, then how can the building be rightly corrected? Not easily, if at all.

## 2• Preparation: Readying your heart.

Once one knows it is God's will to get married, then each person needs to work hard on eliminating as many spiritual problems they have in their lives. Many of the more serious problems should have already been brought to the surface. Others might yet come to the surface. I am still facing problems in my life that I didn't know were there earlier in my life. I have contaminated my marriage and children with such attitudes.

Isaiah 40:1-5 shows the process of discipleship where we need to get rid of the things that shouldn't be there in life. Pride, bitterness, anger or divisive are just a few of these examples. There are other problems too such as incurred debt that puts a lot of pressure on the marriage and should be eliminated as much as possible. Other things like fear, anxiety, stress, doubt, etc. destroy the ability to take hold of the beautiful things that God has given the married couple.

In many cases, as the courting couple discusses different issues, they will discover that they have wrongly responded and sometimes imitated their parents evil words, attitudes and deeds. This frequently happens after visiting their parents. The couple should take an inventory and begin working on it, keeping one another accountable. At this stage, the man might consider not being too frank about sexual lusts and instead have a pastor, father or brother that keeps him accountable.

For every problem area, think of it as a target that must be shot down. God wants none of these things in our lives. Through the power of the cross of Christ, we have forgiveness and through the working of the Holy Spirit, He enables us to overcome the sins grasping onto our souls. We need to be godly men and women in order to have a blessed marriage.

You might wonder, what is acceptable? We learn that no bitterness, no wrath, no anger, etc. is our standard. We look at the scripture and accept that as our standard. We make no excuses, but instead repent. Look at this passage below on what should be put aside and what attitudes and behaviors should be adopted. As a couple memorizes this passage, they should go through each phrase and in love evaluate how they are doing. Even better, though much more difficult, ask your partner how are you doing!

> *"Therefore, laying aside falsehood, SPEAK TRUTH, EACH ONE of you, WITH HIS NEIGHBOR, for we are members of one another. BE ANGRY, AND yet DO NOT SIN; do not let the sun go down on your anger, and do not give the devil an opportunity. Let him who steals steal no longer; but rather let him labor, performing with his own hands what is good, in order that he may have something to share with him who has need."*

> *"Let no unwholesome word proceed from your mouth, but only such a word as is good for edification according to the need of the moment, that it may give grace to those who hear. And do not grieve the Holy Spirit of God, by whom you were sealed for the day of redemption. Let all bitterness and wrath and anger and clamor and slander be put away from you, along with all malice. And be kind to one another, tender-hearted, forgiving each other, just as God in Christ also has forgiven you"* (Ephesians 4:25-32).

We are not saying that we can get all these sins totally out of our lives, but when we get serious, we can go a long way in eliminating different kinds of sins. Anything evil that is not eliminated, will plague our marriage and family until it is eliminated. God's will is holiness. Our goal is to get rid of all known sin by His grace and for His glory dedicate ourselves and bodies to serving His glory.

Couples talk a lot about love, but most do not know about love but only infatuation. They are thinking only how the other one fulfills their needs. A couple needs to put away sins which keep them from truly loving and start focusing on serving the other's needs.

A by-product of this pursuit of godliness in the premarital stage results in wonderful, genuine, honest and humble conversations. My wife and I had many of these discussions. I wish we had more. We were so spiritual immature in some aspects that we couldn't even see so many sins. But others thankfully were being dealt with. A guy, for example, must realize that unless he puts away sexual lusts and fantasies, then he is not going to be a faithful husband but an adulterous one (at least in mind)! Since those early Bible studies and open discussions, we have continued on in these same type of discussions and prayer times. Put down good roots and let them sink deep into the soil of life.

## 3• The Plan: Becoming a Christ-centered home.

Couples are couple-oriented. They are caught up in the exciting potential of being and living together. We don't want to dampen these hopes but put them in the right perspective. A couple must not think of themselves as being autonomous. They should not think of their home to be a place for them alone, but for Christ and His purposes. These dreams need to be interlocked early on before marriage so that everything is placed on a firm foundation.

We must reject the popular notions that a couple lives for itself. If the Lord is calling a couple together, then He is calling them together to serve Him. The couple must think before marriage on how God has gifted them and then anticipate how God will use them together as one unit.

We need to get practical. We see many couples spending so much money on a wedding. They need to be careful for even this can be idolatrous. They spend so much effort and money on a wedding and honeymoon that they go into debt! Surely this is not God's will. Simple is better. Getting a clearer focus on how God wants them to live out their lives for Him is more important. Have a wonderful time planning for your marriage but be simple. Only focus more time on being better prepared. The wedding only establishes your oneness before God. It will not make you one of heart.

We were happy only to have snacks rather than a meal. We went to a humble honeymoon place and had a wonderful time. We didn't have much money. We had things we wanted to do after marriage. So we went simple. A couple must talk early on about their expectations of the wedding. Many of them are conjured up from bridal magazines rather than the scriptures. Christ is to be the center of our weddings.

Christ is also to be the center of one's new home. This means that the couple will regularly pray together. This does not allow for the man to only pray quietly. He must pray aloud and lead the family close to Christ. Each partner will have their own quiet times. How does it work out practically? Let me share what we have and still do almost 25 years into our marriage. It is wonderful how it enables us to share and live out our lives together.

- Dad and Mom are up first early in the morning having their own private devotional times.

- Now that we have children, we also have a devotional time together with the children on most mornings around the breakfast table. We pray, sing, read a passage of scripture (usually Proverbs or Psalm). We added this later on but have found it very important to putting the day before the Lord.

- We pray at meal times.

- After dinner, we have evening devotions (family altar). This is longer then the morning time. We sing together a hymn or sing a song or two, memorize scripture together, or read scripture. We used to memorize a child's catechism (question and answer), but later found it more effective to ask questions around the scripture that we are going over. And we pray. We pray for family needs, but also for missionaries and people in need. If I have a meeting, my wife leads.

- Later in the night, my wife and I meet together. We usually end up talking 1/2 hour to an hour (and sometimes more!) and then pray about what we just discussed. This has developed from our early premarital Bible study and prayer times.

To be Christ-centered, we need to love Christ and His Word more than all. We are not legalistic about these things, but do it because we know it is best. We are not law-centered but Christ-centered. He is the reason we live, and so we must carefully live our lives around what He wants. If He wants us to give 10% and more of our income, then we do it, even though we might have other special needs. Christ first. A Christ-centered marriage is one that sets communication with God and each other as a priority. We carefully govern what we think, say and do according to His purposes. Each decision needs to be based on scriptural principles.

We must love His people and regularly be involved in a local church. If there is a small group, we should be there. It is best not to date when a young man and woman are together alone. That increases wrong expectations and creates special temptations. We recommend for those looking for a possible marriage partner to court under the guidance of their parents.

# 4• Team work: One Heart and Mind.

We all read about Adam and Eve being one, but rarely is it fulfilled in the lives of the average married couple. In order to have one mind and heart, it is not only important for a husband to lovingly lead his wife according to God's Word, and the wife to faithfully submit to him, but also for them both to have the same mindset. There are two evils that must be avoided.

1) In some cultures, one might not think the wife needs to know much about what the husband is thinking. The husband is the dominant leader and the wife is expected and trained to obey. While this is not the modern Western model, it is for many cultures. The problem is not the husband carrying out his leadership position or the wife submitting to the husband. That is true. But if we stop here, we miss out on the most beautiful interlocking of souls that is possible.

The Lord wants the wife to be a husband's 'help meet'. We do not see this only meaning that the wife takes cares of all the laundry and meals. In Genesis 2 we see them share life together. God has made woman differently; she is finely tuned to circumstances and people's feelings. God made her to help 'her' man excel as well as to care for children. If a woman is to make a true contribution to life, then she needs to know what is going on.

The husband needs to cultivate such a talking relationship where she understands what he is wrestling with, and so that he understands her and can listen to her insights. So often husbands do not believe that wives have anything to contribute. With this mindset, he will not share with her. God made it so that man cannot excel without his wife's wisdom. If the husband really loves her, then he will open his soul to her. The wife will respond wonderfully to this. In the end, the wife still must trust her husband to make the final decision, but at least she knows he has heard and values her opinion.

2) In other cultures such as our modern Western culture, women are trained to be independent and rebellious to authority. They are taught to assert themselves rather than to be gentle and quiet-spirited. Couples like this end up being so far from being of one mind and heart. They might live together, but they work and live their own lives. Some don't even live together!

The couple needs to get back to biblical living where a couple is not one in name only but also in practical ways. Communication is important because it is here that a couple needs to come to common understanding. The only easy way to do this is to have a common perspective. Our goal is that the couple regularly make godly decisions. They have come to agree what God wants and encourages each other to do what God wants. I (Paul) have found that when my faith is strong, it helps her. But when my faith is quivering, my wife's faith is strong and vibrant. I remember not a few time when we were very tight on money. My wife would always make out the check to the church first. I felt I would probably wait a bit. But her confidence brought her to write the check, something we both agreed we should do. (We have discussed how to do this in another article).

Making biblical decisions is the goal but a extra bonus is the uniting of the hearts and minds of the husband and wife. We want to see them both love things that God loves. If this is true, then the decision become much easier.

# 5• The Vision: Making plans for the future.

We find it very helpful when considering marriage to think where one wants to go. As one begins to answer this question, ask yourselves, "What is it that God wants for you as a family?" You will find that you have different answers, and if not different answers, you will have different emphases. However, we will discover that many things which we think is so important now will not be that important later on.

We only have so much strength and time. We need to focus on what is good and lovely. We need to purpose ourselves to do God's will. In most cases, God wants to develop a big family. God emphasizes this in a number of places. Unfortunately, family planning practices that are propagated today are not at all trying to understand what God wants. They largely stem from three kinds of people:

➡ (1) Those who are trying to limit the wrong people from being born,

➡ (2) Those who believe that man is ruining the earth, and

➡ (3) Those who think children are too expensive and interfere with their preferred lifestyle.

The Christian church has got involved in this affair with the world. They do not think of their families with a sense of priority but only their careers and wealth. How unfortunate! They see birth control and even abortion in some cases as a means to get where they want to go. They have their goals clearly guiding them. But they are not God's goals of building a godly family.

God wants big families for the most part. Even after the flood, God tells Noah to multiply and fill the earth. People joke that the earth is already full, but it hardly is. People no longer believe God can care for lots of people. God designed it so that it could care for a great multitude. This is God's goal. Just think, do you honestly believe it is right for others to have many children who are brought up in different religions and beliefs while Christians limit themselves to one or two? Is this God's goal?

Of course, God is not just interested in lots of children. He is interested in godly children. Parents must put their toys away and get serious in this task of raising godly children. It has nothing to do with the children but everything to do with what the parents do. Don't believe what you hear! We are not to raise children to make decisions for themselves! We are to raise children to submit to authority and listen to the guidance of parents and God's Word.

If the wife has a career. She should give it up. If she insists on maintaining a career, then she should honestly ask if she really should get married. We have to think down the road as to the implications of our decisions. It is wrong to avoid having children so to carry on our career. But neither is it right for women to have children but have their heart elsewhere. Resentment will build up and the children will not feel loved. Feminism has confused many a Christian woman. It is time these women arise and live by God's Word.

> *"An excellent wife is the crown of her husband,*
> *But she who shames him is as rottenness in his*
> *bones" (Proverbs 12:4, NASB).*

The man, too, must catch the vision of leading the family and not just follow along. The problem is that often he just ignores the wife and family and continues on with his career. He thinks that his job is to make money. We see nothing like this in the Bible. Read Proverbs 1-4, and one will see how the father counseled the son. Read Deuteronomy 6 and see the responsibility to carefully shepherd his children. If we are going to raise godly children, we need to make those right commitments in our soul.

God's will is to take God's Word and wrestle it into ones soul until one has no other passion than to do our Father's will. Holiness requires a separation from our culture where its evil tentacles have lurched onto us. We must repent and prioritize God's will and way. This alone is considered worship.

*****

We have discussed five areas that need to be focused on. Many other things can be discussed. We hope a godly pastor and his wife can mentor you through premarital counseling.[3]

---

[3] Check out the Marriage Navigator that has many free articles on marriage: www.foundationsforfreedom.net/Topics/Marriage/MarriageOverview.html

# Appendix 3: About the Author

After cross-cultural church planting and pastoring for the first two decades of his ministry, the Lord led Paul to establish *Biblical Foundations for Freedom* in 2000. When serving God's people, Paul began to be sensitized to the need for good biblical and yet practical resources to build up the people of God. Since then he has been actively writing, holding international Christian leadership training seminars and serving in the local church.

Paul has been married for more than thirty-five wonderful years. With eight children and three grandchildren, Paul and his wife Linda continually see God's blessings unfold in their lives.

Paul's wide range of materials on Christian life, discipleship, godly living, leadership training, marriage, parenting, anxiety, Old and New Testament and other spiritual life topics provide special insights that are blended into his many books and training materials.

For more on Paul and Linda and the BFF ministry, check online at : www.foundationsforfreedom.net

www.ingramcontent.com/pod-product-compliance
Lightning Source LLC
LaVergne TN
LVHW021401080426
835508LV00020B/2395